COMMUNITY · CONNECTIONS

?

HOW DO THEY HELP?
YMCA
BY KATIE MARSICO

Published in the United States of America by Cherry Lake Publishing
Ann Arbor, Michigan
www.cherrylakepublishing.com

Content Adviser: Rob Fischer, Ph.D., Professor and Director, Master of Nonprofit
Organizations, Jack, Joseph, and Morton Mandel School of Applied Social Sciences,
Case Western Reserve University
Reading Adviser: Marla Conn MS, Ed., Literacy specialist, Read-Ability, Inc.

Photo Credits: © Wavebreakmedia/istock, cover, 1, 17; © Lisa F. Young/Shutterstock, 5;
© Susan Chiang/istock, 7, 15; © Jupiterimages/Thinkstock, 9; © Jack Moebes/CORBIS, 11;
© Bryanpollard | Dreamstime.com - YMCA At UNC-Chapel Hill Photo, 13;
© Kzenon/Shutterstock, 19; © goodluz/Shutterstock, 21

LIBRARY OF CONGRESS CATALOGING-IN-PUBLICATION DATA
Names: Marsico, Katie, 1980- author.
Title: YMCA / by Katie Marsico.
Description: Ann Arbor : Cherry Lake Publishing, 2016. |
Series: Community connections: How do they help? | Audience: K to Grade 3. |
  Includes bibliographical references and index.
Identifiers: LCCN 2015048736| ISBN 9781634710565 (hardcover) |
  ISBN 9781634711555 (pdf) | ISBN 9781634712545 (pbk.) |
  ISBN 9781634713535 (ebook)
Subjects: LCSH: Charities—Juvenile literature. | Charities—Management—Juvenile literature. |
  Young Men's Christian associations—History—Juvenile literature.
Classification: LCC HV40 .M3867 2016 | DDC 267/.3—dc23 LC record available
at http://lccn.loc.gov/2015048736

Cherry Lake Publishing would like to acknowledge the
work of The Partnership for 21st Century Learning.
Please visit www.p21.org for more information.

Printed in the United States of America
Corporate Graphics
CLFA11

CONTENTS

PUSHING FOR POSITIVE CHANGE

Roughly one in four children in the United States grows up without learning how to read. As adults, they face several challenges. For instance, **illiteracy** is linked to problems such as unemployment, **poverty**, and crime.

Yet the YMCA (Young Men's Christian Association) proves that it's never too late to learn. Adult literacy

The ability to read is one of the most important skills a person can have.

Are you able to guess how widespread adult illiteracy is? Sadly, it's more common than you might think. In the United States alone, 44 million adults report being unable to read to their children.

5

programs are just one example of how the YMCA sparks positive changes in people's lives.

The YMCA is a **nonprofit** organization with branches in 125 countries. One of its goals involves offering people opportunities to learn and succeed. Another goal focuses on supporting good health through programs that encourage fitness and safety. Finally, the YMCA provides **social services** that address problems such as unemployment and substance abuse.

Playing basketball is fun! It also helps you stay healthy and builds teamwork.

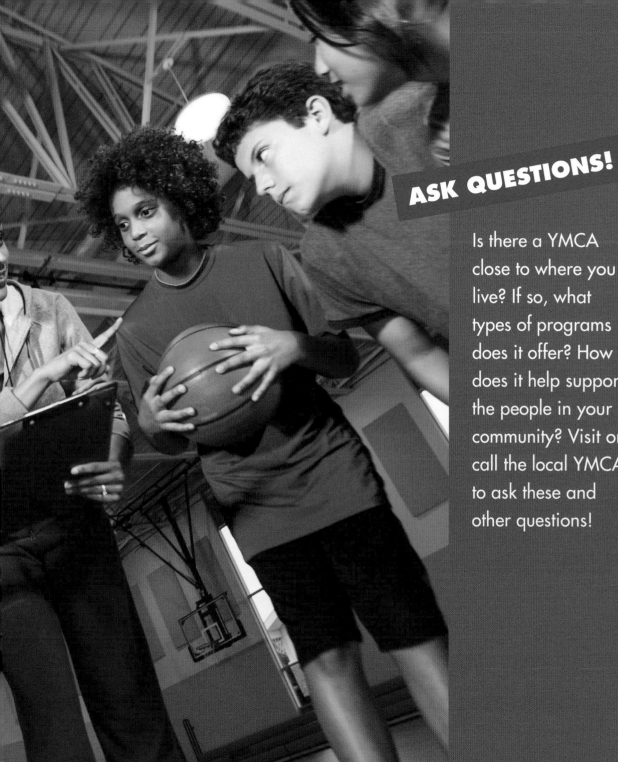

Is there a YMCA close to where you live? If so, what types of programs does it offer? How does it help support the people in your community? Visit or call the local YMCA to ask these and other questions!

7

FROM THE PAST TO THE PRESENT

George Williams created the earliest branch of the YMCA in London, England, in 1844. At that time, the city was filled with young men searching for jobs. Many of them were far from home and were not used to London's sometimes dangerous streets. As a result, they often turned to alcohol and other unhealthy activities.

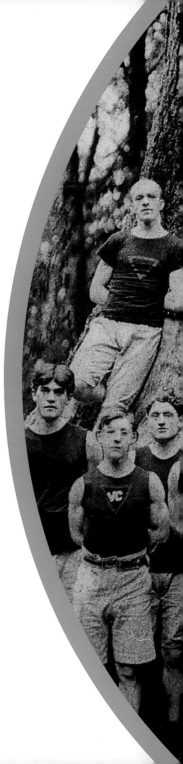

The original goal of the YMCA was to help young men succeed.

Go online or head to the library to look for pictures of London in the mid-1800s. Do you see a lot of factories? Look for clues that reveal some of the social challenges residents faced during that period in history.

Williams founded the YMCA to provide such men with more options. At first, the organization was mainly a Bible study and prayer group. As time passed, the YMCA began providing a wider variety of services. These included short-term housing, use of a gymnasium, and language classes for immigrants. Decades later, the YMCA continues to support people's growth, health, and social needs.

One of the YMCA's core programs hosts summer camps for children.

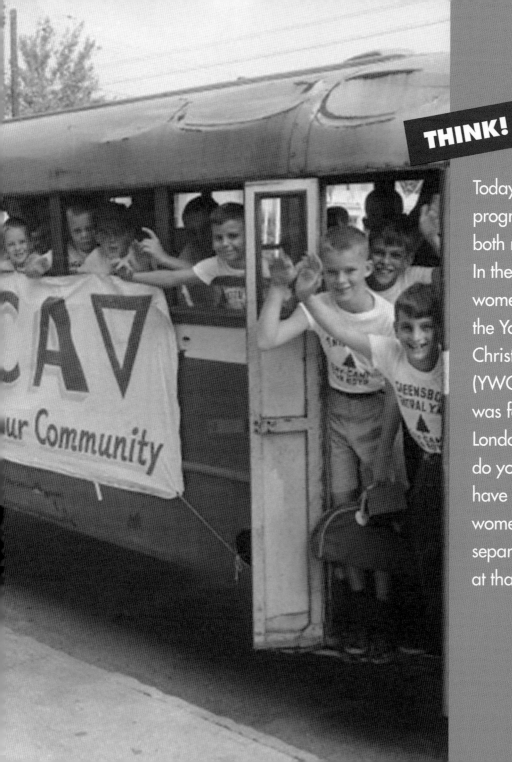

Today, YMCA programming benefits both men and women. In the 1800s, however, women often relied on the Young Women's Christian Association (YWCA). The YWCA was founded in London in 1855. Why do you think it would have been helpful to women to have this separate organization at that time?

11

The YMCA operates based on the idea that everyone deserves a chance to succeed. As a result, its programming benefits individuals of all ages and backgrounds. It offers people the chance to make positive choices and improve their lives. During the next few decades, volunteers started forming branches of the YMCA in other countries.

Today, there are YMCAs all over the world.

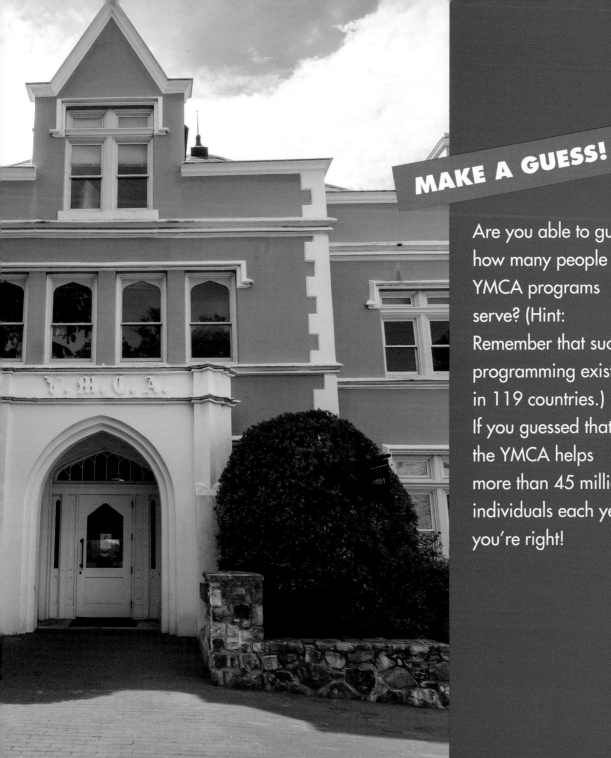

Are you able to guess how many people YMCA programs serve? (Hint: Remember that such programming exists in 119 countries.) If you guessed that the YMCA helps more than 45 million individuals each year, you're right!

13

In order to accomplish its goals, the YMCA relies on a combination of volunteers and paid employees. Many work as coaches, fitness trainers, or staff at child care programs and children's camps. Some offer job skills or teach classes that help participants improve their reading abilities. Others coordinate housing and recovery programs for people struggling with issues such as poverty and **addiction**.

Many YMCA centers have gyms that members can use. Fitness classes are often taught by volunteers.

Are you a member of the YMCA? If not, what must you do to become a member? What are the benefits of membership? Contact your local YMCA to figure out the answers to these questions!

15

SUPPORTING SUCCESS

Many YMCA programs are geared toward helping young people learn and develop. The YMCA oversees camps, child care programs, swimming lessons, and sports and fitness classes. It also provides tutoring, volunteer opportunities, and **mentorship** programs. These activities build confidence and other qualities that a person needs to become a leader.

Swim classes at the YMCA teach children and adults a very important skill.

LOOK!

Head online to look for photographs of different YMCA facilities. Do you notice any features that they have in common? (For example, several YMCA buildings include a gym, pool, and fitness center.)

Of course, the YMCA supports the well-being of people of *all* ages. In some cases, this means educating families about the value of a balanced diet, exercise, and time together. In other cases, YMCA staff and volunteers work with residents to create healthier, safer communities. They try to find solutions to problems ranging from childhood **obesity** to tobacco use.

Classes like this one help the YMCA boost member well-being and community ties.

The YMCA believes that learning new things and staying active are important parts of healthy living. So, it offers everything from Bible study sessions to pottery and cooking classes. Do you think such programs support a person's well-being? If so, how?

The YMCA also teaches people how to be socially responsible. It offers literacy classes, job training, temporary housing, and various types of **counseling**. It also raises awareness about issues involving children, health, and education.

Thanks to the YMCA, individuals and communities across the globe are changing for the better. This organization shows people how to succeed and support each other along the way.

Job training helps people learn new skills and find more rewarding careers.

Create a YMCA calendar. Find out what's happening at your local YMCA next month. Then draw 30 to 31 squares on poster board. Write a date in each, along with a description of events on those dates. Share your calendar with your family!

GLOSSARY

addiction (uh-DIK-shuhn) the state of depending on a substance such as a drug in order to function

counseling (KOUN-suhl-ing) guidance from trained professionals that helps people solve various personal and social problems

illiteracy (ih-LIH-tuh-ruh-see) the state of not knowing how to read or write

mentorship (MEN-tor-ship) a relationship in which someone with more experience offers guidance and advice to someone with less experience

nonprofit (nahn-PRAH-fit) not existing for the main purpose of earning more money than is spent

obesity (oh-BEE-suh-tee) the condition of being extremely overweight

poverty (PAH-vur-tee) the state of being poor

social services (SO-shuhl SUR-vis-iz) programming that benefits a community in areas such as housing, education, and health care

FIND OUT MORE

BOOKS

Cohn, Jessica. *Improving Communities*. Huntington Beach, CA: Teacher Created Materials, 2013.

Henneberg, Susan. *Defeating Addiction and Alcoholism*. New York: Rosen Publishing Group, Inc., 2016.

Marsico, Katie. *Exercise!* Ann Arbor, MI: Cherry Lake Publishing, 2015.

WEB SITES

KidsHealth—Staying Healthy
kidshealth.org/kid/stay_healthy/
Check out links to several online articles about the importance of getting and staying fit!

The YMCA—Youth Development
www.ymca.net/youth-development
This site features short videos and articles about YMCA programming for children and teenagers.

INDEX

ABOUT THE AUTHOR

Katie Marsico is the author of more than 200 children's books. She lives in a suburb of Chicago, Illinois, with her husband and children.